AR
RL 4.1
Pts. 0.5

AR
RL 4.1
Pts. 0.5

GREEK MYTHS

JASON AND THE ARGONAUTS

A RETELLING BY
JESSICA GUNDERSON

ILLUSTRATED BY
NADINE TAKVORIAN

PICTURE WINDOW BOOKS
a capstone imprint

CAST OF CHARACTERS

ORACLE (OR-ack-uhl): priest or priestess through whom a god or goddess speaks

PELIAS (PAY-lee-uhs): king of Iolcos, a city in ancient Greece

HERA (HAIR-uh): goddess of marriage, known for her jealousy

POSEIDON (puh-SY-duhn): god of the sea

JASON (JAY-suhn): nephew of King Pelias; became captain of the *Argo*

ARGOS (AR-gohss): builder of the ship, the *Argo*

ARGONAUTS (AR-goh-nots): the *Argo's* crew

ZETES (ZAY-teez) AND CALAIS (kAl-AY-uhss): winged brothers

PHINEUS (FIN-ee-uhss): king of Salmydessus, who was blind and could see the future

HARPIES (HAR-peez): winged female creatures

AEËTES (ee-EE-teez): king of Colchis and keeper of the Golden Fleece

APHRODITE (a-FRUH-DY-tee): goddess of love

MEDEA (MUH-DEE-uh): sorceress; daughter of Aeëtes

WORDS TO KNOW

COLCHIS—an ancient region at the eastern end of the Black Sea

IOLCOS—an ancient city in central-eastern Greece

MOUNT OLYMPUS—home of the Olympian gods

SACRIFICE—an offering to a god

SORCERESS—a woman who practices magic; also called a witch

THE ORACLE WARNED KING PELIAS

of Iolcos, "Beware of the man with one sandal."

Pelias knew he hadn't been a good king. He'd stolen the throne from his half-brother. And he often ignored the gods, especially Hera. But to beware of a man with one sandal? The king laughed. Who would wear only one sandal?

The king began preparing a sacrifice for Poseidon, the god of the sea. Hera was furious when she heard the king gave offerings to Poseidon but not to her. She knew she must destroy King Pelias. And she had an idea.

Far from the palace, the king's nephew Jason was sleeping. Hera leaned over him and whispered into his ear, "The throne is rightfully yours."

When Jason woke, he was angry. The throne was his! He set off on the long journey to King Pelias' palace.

When Jason reached the River Anaurus, he saw an old woman begging to be carried across. "I'll carry you," Jason offered.

He lifted the woman onto his back. She looked light, but she was heavy—very heavy. Halfway across the river, Jason stumbled and fell. When he stood up, the old woman was gone. And so was his sandal.

Above him, the goddess Hera giggled. She shook herself out of the old woman disguise, holding the sandal in her hand.

King Pelias of Iolcos was sitting on his throne, admiring his riches, when his nephew Jason appeared. The king stood to greet him, then saw that Jason wore only one sandal. He stared at Jason thoughtfully. "What would you do if you knew someone meant to harm you?" he asked.

Jason scowled at the king. What sort of greeting was this? "I'd send him to fetch the Golden Fleece," he answered, surprising himself. He did not realize that Hera, invisible, was again whispering in his ear.

King Pelias smiled. The Golden Fleece! He'd heard much about the fleece. It was the pure-gold coat of a magical ram. It hung in Colchis, a faraway land, and was guarded by a dragon that paced, snarled, and never slept. "Come to think of it, I have always wanted the Golden Fleece," Pelias answered. "I command you to fetch it for me!"

Jason knew there was no point in arguing. "If I get the Golden Fleece, you will hand over the throne," he demanded.

Pelias nodded. "I will," he agreed. But he knew there was no way Jason would succeed at such an impossible task.

Jason called upon the shipbuilder Argos to build him a ship. He named it the *Argo*.

Then he gathered 50 of the strongest and bravest men in Greece to sail to Colchis with him. Among them were fighters, sailors, athletes, and musicians, and even the flying brothers Zetes and Calais.

Jason and his men, called the Argonauts, set sail under a bright sun. The quest for the Golden Fleece had begun.

Jason and the Argonauts sailed for many years in search of Colchis, stopping at places for food and rest. Each place held a new adventure. But as the ship sailed farther from home, Jason worried they'd never find Colchis.

Jason and the Argonauts sailed on until landing at Salmydessus, where a blind, starved king named Phineus greeted them. Gruesome winged creatures hovered above the king, licking their lips.

"Those vicious Harpies steal my food every time I sit down to eat," Phineus moaned.

"We will rid you of the Harpies," Jason promised, "if you tell us the way to Colchis."

When Phineus agreed, Zetes and Calais, the winged brothers, flew quickly into the sky. They chased the Harpies so far away they'd never return.

Phineus told Jason the way to Colchis but warned of the Clashing Rocks. The giant cliffs crashed together and destroyed any ship that tried to pass through. "Release a dove," Phineus told him, "and if it returns unharmed, the passage is open. If not, you must turn back."

Jason and the Argonauts sailed on, and soon they heard the thunderous clashing of the rocks. Fog hung like thick drapes over the cliffs. Jason released a dove high into the air. Then he waited.

At last the dove returned, and Jason and the Argonauts sailed through the cliffs to Colchis.

Aeëtes, the king of Colchis, was not pleased when he heard of the strangers' arrival. He knew there was only one reason anyone would travel so far—to capture the Golden Fleece.

The king frowned when Jason presented himself. "I will not allow you to take my fleece," he told Jason, "unless you earn it."

"How will I do that?" asked Jason.

The king pointed outdoors. In the courtyard, two enormous bulls kicked and bucked. Flames sprayed from their mouths.

"You must harness these bulls and attach a plow to them, without getting burned," the king said.

Jason nodded bravely, but inside he shivered.

"Then you will plow until you uncover the magical dragon's tooth buried in the courtyard," the king continued.

Jason nodded again, watching the kicking bulls breathe fire at him. "How will I ever make it out of Colchis alive?" he wondered.

The goddess Hera had been hiding behind the curtains, watching King Aeëtes speak to Jason. She knew Jason needed help. She flew away and called upon Aphrodite, the goddess of love.

Aphrodite followed Hera to Colchis. As the two goddesses hovered over the land, Aphrodite saw a young woman walking along the river toward the palace. Aphrodite swooped closer to watch her.

The young woman was Medea, the king's daughter. Aphrodite smiled and aimed her bow, shooting an arrow of love into Medea's heart.

At that moment, Medea turned and looked at the palace. She saw Jason standing at the window. Feelings of love pulsed through her heart.

Medea knew what her father had in store for him. If she didn't help Jason, he would surely die.

That night Medea sent messengers who told Jason to meet her by the river. As she watched him approach, she felt the stirrings of love all over again.

"I can help you harness the bulls," she told him.

"You?" he asked with a laugh. "How?"

"Don't laugh," Medea said. "I am also a sorceress." She held out a small vial. "Rub this potion on your body, shield, and sword. It will keep the fire from burning you."

"And what of the dragon's tooth?" Jason asked.

"When you dig up the tooth, armed men will spring from the ground," Medea answered. "Throw stones at them. They will become confused and attack each other instead."

"What can I give you in return?" Jason asked.

Medea smiled. "You will take me as your wife," she said.

"If I succeed, I will marry you," Jason agreed.

The next day, all the people of Colchis gathered to watch the spectacle.

In his room, Jason rubbed Medea's potion all over his body, sword, and shield. He filled a small bag with stones. Then he strode out into the courtyard. He waved at the crowd, the king, and Medea. He even waved at the bulls, who were charging toward him, breathing fire.

As the bulls neared, Jason pretended to dodge the flames. The crowd cheered. Then he marched straight toward the bulls and began dancing in their fire. The heat didn't bother him.

The people were amazed at Jason's bravery. Their cheers grew louder.

Only King Aeëtes sat silent and angry. Next to him, Medea covered her smile.

The bulls grunted and kicked, confused, as Jason looped harnesses over their heads.

King Aeëtes grew angrier still. "But he won't be prepared for the armed men," he thought, consoling himself.

Jason led the bulls around the courtyard. The plow dug deep into the earth. Then he heard a clank as the plow hit the dragon's tooth. He uncovered the tooth and lifted it from the ground, holding it up for the crowd to see. But he kept one hand on the bag filled with stones.

Dozens of armed men suddenly sprang from the ground, their armor and weapons full of soil. Jason hurled one stone, then another, and another.

The men stopped, confused. "Why did you throw a stone at me?" one man shouted to another.

"Why did you throw a stone at *me*?" the man answered, raising his weapon.

All the armed men started shouting and charging toward each other. Jason leaped out of the way to let them fight.

With the fighters occupied, Jason strode toward the surprised and angry king. "I have done what you wished," he said. "Now you must give me what I want: the Golden Fleece!"

"Never!" cried King Aeëtes.

"Never!" Medea cried in agreement. But as Jason turned away, she whispered, "Meet me near the fleece. Hurry!"

The fleece hung shimmering and golden from the trees. A dragon larger than the *Argo* itself paced around the fleece, hissing and spitting.

"How will I fend off the gigantic dragon?" Jason wondered.

Medea laughed. "I'm a sorceress, remember?" she said. She began chanting, and the dragon calmed. Medea stepped forward and sprinkled a potion over its eyes. The dragon dropped off to sleep.

Jason quickly gathered up the Golden Fleece. He and Medea ran toward the ship where the Argonauts waited, oars ready.

King Aeëtes and his men followed the *Argo*, but their ships weren't fast enough. Jason and the Argonauts sailed into the horizon, bound for Iolcos. With his victorious quest for the Golden Fleece, Jason thought he would soon become king.

When Jason returned to Iolcos, he marched straight to King Pelias' palace. When Pelias saw Jason, he paled. He hadn't expected Jason to return, especially not with the Golden Fleece.

"I am king now," said Jason.

"Never!" cried the king. "Be gone with him!" Pelias' guards forced Jason out of the palace and warned him never to come back.

When she learned what the king had said, Medea was angry. She wanted Jason to be king, and herself to be queen. She would make Pelias pay.

Medea told Pelias' daughters that she had a potion to make their old father young and strong again. But first they had to slice him into pieces. She demonstrated by sprinkling potion on the pieces of an old ram, which immediately sprang to life, young and beautiful.

The princesses chopped up their father. But after he was in pieces, Medea threw away the potion and left Pelias for dead.

Now no one stood between Jason and the throne.

But Medea didn't foresee the anger of the frightened people of Iolcos. As punishment for the murder, they forced Jason and Medea to leave the country, warning them never to return. Jason would never become king.

Jason's quest wasn't fulfilled as he had planned, but there was one who was quite pleased with the turn of events. From high above the clouds on Mount Olympus, the goddess Hera smiled. Pelias had received the ultimate punishment for ignoring her. Hera had gotten her revenge.

READ MORE

Daly, Kathleen N. and revised by Marian Rengel. *Greek and Roman Mythology, A to Z*. New York: Chelsea House Publishers, 2009.

Limke, Jeff. *Jason: Quest for the Golden Fleece*. Graphic Myths and Legends. Minneapolis: Graphic Universe, 2007.

Yomtov, Nel, retold by. *Jason and the Golden Fleece*. Graphic Revolve. Minneapolis: Stone Arch Books, 2009.

INTERNET SITES

FactHound offers a safe, fun way to find Internet sites related to this book. All of the sites on FactHound have been researched by our staff.

Here's all you do:

Visit *www.facthound.com*

Type in this code: 9781404866690

Super-cool stuff! Check out projects, games and lots more at www.capstonekids.com

LOOK FOR ALL THE BOOKS IN THE GREEK MYTHS SERIES:

THE BATTLE OF THE OLYMPIANS AND THE TITANS

JASON AND THE ARGONAUTS

MEDUSA'S STONY STARE

ODYSSEUS AND THE CYCLOPS

PANDORA'S VASE

THE WOO...

Thanks to our adviser for his expertise and advice:
Terry Flaherty, PhD
Professor of English
Minnesota State University, Mankato

Editor: Shelly Lyons
Designer: Alison Thiele
Art Director: Nathan Gassman
Production Specialist: Sarah Bennett
The illustrations in this book were created with pencil.

Picture Window Books
1710 Roe Crest Drive
North Mankato, MN 56003
www.capstonepub.com

All books published by Picture Window Books are manufactured with paper containing at least 10 percent post-consumer waste.

Library of Congress Cataloging-in-Publication Data
Gunderson, Jessica.
Jason and the argonauts : a retelling / by Jessica Gunderson; illustrated by Nadine Takvorian.
p. cm. — (Greek myths)
Includes index.
ISBN 978-1-4048-6669-0 (library binding)
1. Jason (Greek mythology)—Juvenile literature.
2. Argonauts (Greek mythology)—Juvenile literature.
I. Title. II. Series.

BL820.A8G86 2012
398.20938'01—dc22   2011006588

Printed in the United States of America in North Mankato, Minnesota.
122011   006515R